HADITHI ya NAMBARI

THE NUMBER STORY

SMALL BOOK ONE

ENGLISH - SWAHILI

*Numbers Teach Children
Their Number Names*

written and illustrated by

MISS ANNA

Early Reader Edition of *The Number Story 1*
Bronze Medal Winner, 2016 Wishing Shelf Book Award

Library of Congress Control Number: 2018902040

Names: Miss Anna, author.
Title: Number story : numbers teach children their number names / Miss Anna.
Description: Portland, OR: Lumpy Publishing, 2018.
Identifiers: ISBN 978-1-945977-26-8 | LCCN 2018902040
Summary: The pictures and rhymes present stories which introduce numbers 0-10.
Subjects: LCSH Numeration—English--Swahili--Pictorial works--Juvenile literature. | BISAC JUVENILE NONFICTION /
Languages: English--Swahili
Classification: LCC QA141.3 .M57 2018 | DDC 513—dc23

Publisher: Lumpy Publishing
Website: www.missannabooks.com
Email: missanna@missannabooks.com

Paperback: ISBN 978-1-945977-26-8
Printed in the U.S.A.   1 3 5 7 9 10 8 6 4 2

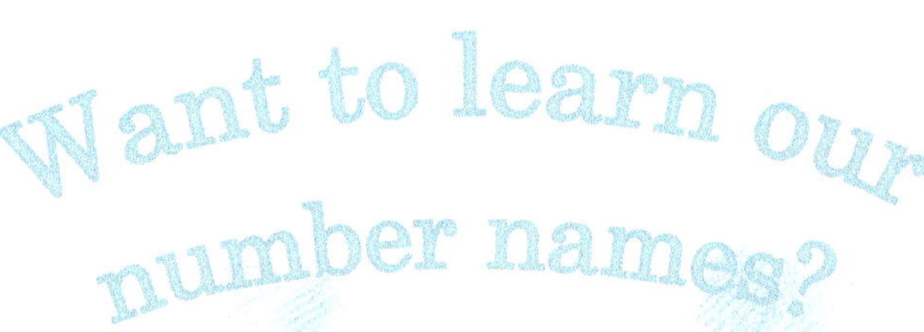

Ungetaka kusoma majina ya nambari?

It is very easy and a lot of fun!

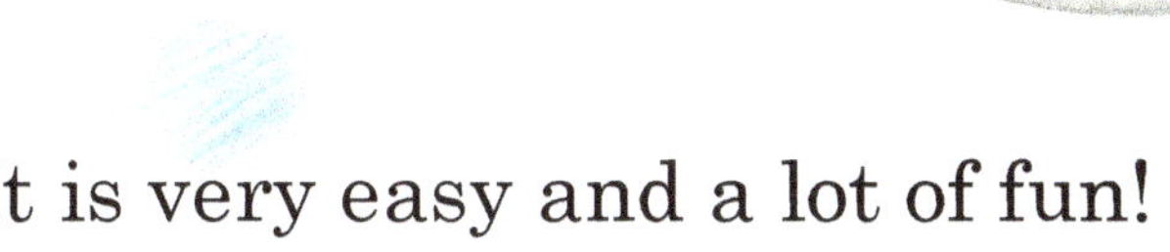

Ni rahisi sana na inafurahisha!

Say-along our little jingle

Rudia nyuma yangu.

starting from Number One!

Kuanzia nambari ya kwanza!

ONE looks like my one finger.

MOJA

Inakaa kama
kidole changu kimoja.

ONE!
MOJA!

2

TWO trails a tail.

MBILI

Inavuta mkia.

A TAIL! MKIA!

3

THREE has bumps.

TATU

Ina matuta.

BUMPY! MATUTA!

4

FOUR carries a sail.

NNE

Ni mashua.

4
A SAIL!
MASHUA!

5
FIVE   is a racing track.
TANO
Ni njia ya mbio.
Ni kufuatilia barabara.

VROOM
VRUUM!
1

SIX curves like a snail.

SITA

Linapinda kama konokono.

A SNAIL! KONOKONO!

7

SEVEN has a sharp angle.

SABA

Lina pembe kali.

OUCH!
UUI!

8

EIGHT   is rollercoaster rails.

NANE

Ni pandashuka.
rollercoaster

HUREE!
YIPPEE!

9

NINE is a bubble on a stick.

TISA

Ni povu nzuri.

bubble

A BUBBLE! NI POVU!

TEN   is an eye of a whale.

KUMI

Ni jicho moja la nyangumi.

WINK!
KONYEZA!

HELLO! JAMBO!

And
NA

0

ZERO is an empty pail.

SUFURI

Ni ndoo tupu.

IT'S EMPTY!
NI TUPU!

Thank you for playing with us today.

We had a lot of fun too!

Asante kwa kucheza nasi leo.

Tulikuwa na wakati mwema pia!

We are your Number friends,
Zero to Ten,
Who will be here for you~
Sisi ni marafiki wenu wa nambari,
sufuri hadi kumi.
Tutakuwa hapa ukituhitaji.

Bye-bye now!
See you again soon!
Kwaheri-Kwaheri sasa!
Tuonane tena hivi karibuni!

The Numbers are *SINGING* too!

To sing-a-long, look for Miss Anna Number Story
at your favorite music store like iTUNES.

MP3

Numbers 0-10
IDENTIFYING
& COUNTING

Numbers 11-20
& Ordinals
first, second, third...

Numbers 0-100
& Place Values
ones, tens, hundreds...

About Clocks
& Telling Time
hours, minutes, seconds...

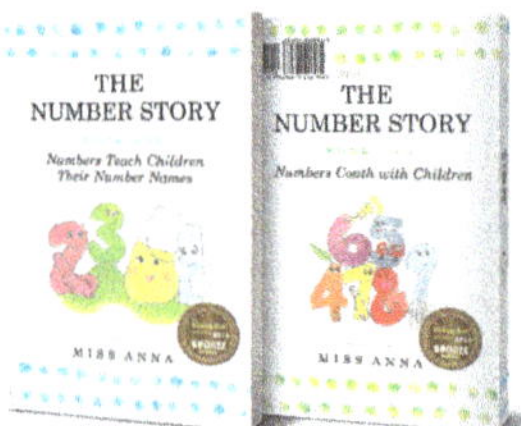

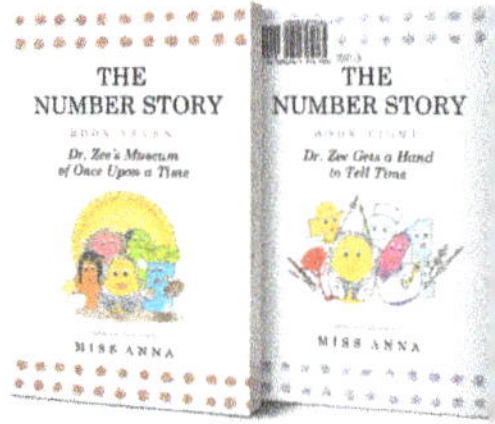

Number Story 1 & 2
isbn: 978-0-996216-48-7

Number Story 3 & 4
isbn: 978-1-945977-01-5

Number Story 5 & 6
isbn: 978-1-945977-06-0

Number Story 7 & 8
isbn: 978-1-949320-40-4

For more Miss Anna books to love,
visit us at

www.missannabooks.com

Numbers are working hard all over the world!
Come Travel the World with Us!